An I Can Read Book®

Who Will Be My Friends?

Story and pictures by

SYD HOFF

Author-artist of DANNY AND THE DINOSAUR

HarperCollins*Publishers*

HarperCollins®, 🏭®, and I Can Read Book®
are trademarks of HarperCollins Publishers Inc.

Library of Congress Catalog Card Number: 60-14096

ISBN 0-06-022556-4 (lib. bdg.)
ISBN 0-06-444072-9 (pbk.)
First Harper Trophy edition, 1985.

10 11 12 13 SCP 10 9 8

Freddy moved into a new house.

He liked his room.

He liked the street.

"Who will be my friends?" he asked.

He rolled his ball to a little dog.

He rolled his ball to a cat.

They did not roll it back.

"Who will be my friends?" he asked.

"I am your friend,"

said the policeman.

"I am your friend,"

said the mailman.

"I am your friend,"

said the street cleaner.

"Let's play ball," said Freddy.

"I have to walk my beat,"

said the policeman.

"I have to bring the mail,"
said the mailman.

"I have to clean the street,"

said the street cleaner.

"Who will be my friends?"

asked Freddy.

He went to the playground.

Boys were playing ball.

"Who will be my friends?"

asked Freddy.

21

The boys went right on playing.

"I guess I will have to play by myself,"

said Freddy.

He threw his ball up in the air—

—and caught it.

He threw his ball up in the air—

—and caught it!

He threw it still higher—

—and caught it!

"Who will be my friends?"

asked Freddy.

"We will," said the boys.

"We need someone who can throw

and catch like that."

31

"Let's shake on it," said Freddy.

And they did.